Two Shades

By

Joseph Siwik

© 2014 Joseph Siwik

First Edition

ISBN: 978-0-692-31904-8

Digital Editions (epub and mobi formats) produce by Booknook.biz

Acknowledgement

Encouragement, thoughtfulness and embracing the world
Positive, supportive and meaningful words
Contributions, inspiration, knowledge and help
Positive morals, creations of wealth.

Patience, guidance, feelings with love
Kindness, friendships, faith and support
A simple thank you is not enough.

Sincere Gratitude

Dedication

A soft voice, a mother's touch
A little note, a rhyme or two
A reader suggests a quote for you
A little creation, a little spark
Stirs my imagination in the dark

A soulful beat, no rhyming feet
A simple standard, I love to read
What I write is what I bleed
A simple poem that's what I see
How inspiration makes me scream
A pen creates my vivid dreams

Pencils and paper travel abroad
A simple note, leaves a golden touch
A little dramatic and a little old
Creates a poem, soon to be told.

From tiny sparks of inspiration
Great things are born
Allowing me to be creative
Teaching me right and wrong
Giving me courage and support

Compassion, understanding and positive gains
Hard work, determination and great faith
Tears of joy run down my face

Leads to a support team I would not change.

Thank you!

Prologue

A city divided with no given mind, needs to put all its prejudices aside. Setting restrictions on who can survive, racial images are being applied, threatening the existence of day and night.

A depth so deep, anger crosses in between making humans weep. A road traveled by many souls, depicts illusions new and old. A simple tale, some blues and soul, keeps the reader going forward in a deceptive world.

J.S.

Contents

Facade 1

   "Tonight You Are Only You" 2

   "Two Shades: Light" 4

   "Downtown" 5

   "Attitudes" 7

   "Second Chance" 8

Surrender 10

   "No Way to Surrender" 11

   "Courtroom Drama" 12

   "Blinded by Truth" 13

   "Gallagher Seed" 14

   "Judgment Day" 16

   "Antiquity" 17

No Solid Ground 18

   "Margaret Steed" 19

   "Patriotism" 21

   "Revenge" 25

   "Racist" 26

   "Black and White" 27

   "Civil War" 29

Isolation 31

   "Suffered" 32

"Solitude" 33

"Deranged and Alone" 34

"A Fool's Outcry" 35

"Deprived of My Senses" 37

"Inner Grief" 38

Reflections of the Dead 39

"Fallen Hero" 40

"Dean Faltz" 43

"What Lies Ahead" 45

"Remorse" 46

"Lost Soul" 48

"Burnt reflections" 49

"Illusions of Innocence" 50

Curtains 51

"Death to My Soul" 52

"Captive" 54

"Goodbye" 55

"Whispers" 56

"Two Shades: Dark" 57

Facade

"Tonight You Are Only You"

Tonight you are only you
Hidden behind a façade
Written are the words you believe
Tonight you are only you

Empty feelings still impair your view
Having no truth to them
Deceitful lies brutalize your mind
Plagued like the city
The streets crumble within
Misery is not your thing
You scream defeat

Brittle yet ugly
Powerful yet different
Grievance is felt

An empty seat
An empty chair
A lost relative is no longer there
A cool soft mist follows within
A dim light appears

The air thick with dust
Creates an illusion so deep
A silent street
A guilty world
Sympathy is never felt

Selfish goals demoralize your veins
Traces of sweet words cinch in your head
A dirty pervert has no common sense

Lies all lies
A dirty night
A midnight walker stalks from behind
A day lost
A dirty deed gone wrong

A city full of shame
Threatens your game
The never ending sorrow
Threatens your shame
Yet you keep a straight face
Blending it smooth
From an old lady to a wandering buffoon
You keep our hearts totally amused
Diversity seems a simple rule

The characters you leave behind
Never seem to gain a prize
Only a laughter or a smile
Amazes no one, just a few

Tonight you are only you
Hidden behind a façade
Written are the words you believe
Until a curtain drops.

"Two Shades: Light"

One dark
One light
One laughs
One cries
One seeks
One defines
One is lonely at night.

"Downtown"

A guilty pleasure
A seductive move
Downtown seems so shady
I do not want to be a lady
How dare they call me lazy?

Portrayed the wrong way
A potential disaster
Actual and artificial rumors spread today

A boss screams
A newspaper prints
A machine on the frits

A dream inspired
An inspiration from above
A little caption moves us along

A vacating town
A neighborhood in disguise
A shadow in the dark
Brings a new attitude

A different point of view
A defining moment
A knife, the weapon of choice
Sends me falling to the ground

Disappointed in myself
Therapy sessions do not help

Total waste of time and hope
How fast one's mood can change
My beliefs are over thrown

If I die today
What would tomorrow bring
Political unrest
No solid ground
Absolute defiance
Swallowed into chaos
Driven by demonic forces

Left, right, no turning back
Power ripped from beneath
Am I not allowed to voice my opinion?
Why should I suffer from it?

Its grand illusions, speak hardly to the mass
There's always a generation gap

My world is collapsing around me
But yet I stay strong
Victory has emerged.

"Attitudes"

Emerging victorious, yet denied the right,
Selfish attitudes ride the tide.
Battered and submerged by cold hearted fools.

White and black flesh steaming with anger,
Raging bullets don't seem to matter.
Memories seen humorous, painful no less,
Totally twisted, is this city of vast.

"Second Chance"

A clear picture no longer rules
A cruel majority rules the coup
Settling in for a score
Drives a human to their core

Imploding jabs left and right
Knocks some senses
Straight out of sight
Leaving no come backs
To be denied

A victory seems too meek
A knockout thrives defeat
A heavy price to be paid
Leaves a fighter losing faith

A thrown in towel turns upside
Displaying blood of a wounded knee
Immorality sets in speed
Local savages stir up the heat
Screaming insults to the weak

No self-control
No self-esteem
No gratitude given
No reason to believe

No pun intended
No given fun

A second chance
Seems slim to none.

Surrender

"No Way to Surrender"

A heart weeps of sadness,
A kid cries again,
Why the pain, for the worst, I cannot stand.

Emotions pour, as souls are lost,
Sweet dreams of heaven float above,
A possession to hold or to admire,
Who are these lovebirds that play such a desire?
On a piano from above, or a harp I shall strung,
With sweet music, a loved one has gone.

Gone where, as far as can be seen
In the wind, fire, or in the wave of the heat,
A little girl was taken from under my feet.

A little from one,
A little from another,
No blossom, no life,
No way to surrender.

"Courtroom Drama"

A dramatic entrance
Led for his arrest
Held in contempt
A lawyer protests

Sanctioned by the Court
Refused by the Bar
This lawyer's sanity was way off from par

Silenced by the Judge
He shook his head
Disbelief was his concern

Emotions ran high
The jury strung by a tie
Defendant was mortified
As his bail was denied

Standing mortified and alone
The Judge gave him some hope

Defeated by his own game
Disappointed by his own shame
Toiled by his play, no one seems amazed.

"Blinded by Truth"

There are many secrets hidden in your lies
Electricity flows through your mind
Blinded by truth, incarcerated by your views
Painful descriptions amuse your solitude

Broken down are your rules
Disguised in words
Divorced from society
Your sensitive side, seems almost uptight.

Plagued by design, intrigued by the mind
You question your stay, something to thrive
Your attitude describes your life as a creature of the night

Circled in sunlight, you define your rights
Lust and desire compel you to fight
You aggravate every soul in sight
You are the torment of our lives.

"Gallagher Seed"

A two faced activist was flooded by truth
His character tells it all, his mood delivers,
His facial features quiver, his breath reeks of lies
His movements seek denial; every idea of his is hated

Dare his racial tensions, he seeks compliance
Not given in society, he evades an existing bullet
His existing poison drains reality
His existence is not so great, how does he do it
One seems to ornate

He was wise, not foolish, spoke eloquently but yet
He mystified everyone in between
Like a ravaged beast on the stand
He spoke like a true gentleman with clear driven motive
Yet he had no illusions, just complete confusion
How wrong was he, one might wonder?
Prosecution could not even win a conviction.

Admission to guilty, no way, he pleads he was framed
Some say there were no promises to be kept
In that small little head
But he had his own way to create delays,
Are people not seeing the same?
The vicious cycle that makes his day
At its best his unique voice coerces the land

A depth of silence came across the air
When he entered the room, all said and done
Who is this old vagabond with so many mistakes?

Along with a deep wooden scent,
Not even the truth shall set him free.

Remorse is something we cannot coerce
Out of an ignorant man
Who decides what he sends
Disgusted by his virtues, we are left to no end.
I foretell the rest, given his death
There is no mercy for an activist laid to rest.

"Judgment Day"

Pleasure, pain, why no gain,
How dare you speak that way?
You a Roman! Yet I laugh,
Is there no shame, in your crying game?

Do you speak the words I recognize?
Bloodhounds give a cry,
Give forth to speak and there you shall reside.

Defying corruption against your shame,
Your lawyer abdicates,
A tense motion accuses the Judge,
Arbitration is the settlement to your lure.

Dear to speak a second word,
For contempt is where you land.
Awkward it shall seem,
With his hands, a free man speaks.

No remorse occupies the length,
Forthcoming is the judgment,
To which some have suffered, in justifying the end.

"Antiquity"

Forgotten and never spoken are the days of old
Leaving so many people seeking hope
Thinking second chances will give a rise
Seeking the future one step at a time

Where does the future hide?
In our thoughts, in our prayers or in our views
In photographs, records, old timers and gold

Like memories, mirrors and reflections of old
In our mind, in our visions, or developing on site
The future is unpredictable given its hold
Its hold on life all seems to unfold
Is that so?
Where does the future seem to roam?
Depicting illusions, not given to me
Revealing great fortunes
Have yet to be seen.

No Solid Ground

"Margaret Steed"

Bare as a tree in winter, was my land
Separated yet equal from the rest
I declared my protest
But against who!

Did I know them?
Did they know me?
Is my life an existence?
Separate but equal in two different worlds
This is my story.

Race does not hate me for who I am
It's the color of my skin that shapes my land
The land I walk on with my bare feet
Why do I not fit in amongst the trees?

So many times I have asked this question
Still pondering an answer, mainly at night
Silence is golden, I wonder why?
Am I even an existence in their lives?

I seem to forget my own shade at times
I realize my color defines my rights
I now realize how much I hate this life
Still pondering, am I an existence in their lives?

The labor, the beatings, the cold hearted killings
My patience is depleting to survive
I still ponder am I an existence in their lives.

There was no me to sacrifice
I would not dare speak at a given time
To whom shall I plea for my life
Am I an existence or just a figure of mind?

Trembled with fear, I dare not ask
I find my tortured feelings deep down inside
That I would not dare speak of this sacrifice
Now I realize my race has died
Seeking to be an existence in their happy lives

Anger rages inside me
For the reasons I cannot say
Depression continues to eat away
If only I could escape
This tormented life would finally decay
And I would be free to express my needs.

Bare as a tree in winter, was my land
Separated yet equal, I finally declared
That a little parcel was finally my share.

"Patriotism"

A new place with a chosen path
A life of fear with a dream of tears
A hidden culture of a promise land
A simple prayer from a decent man
A mirror image of a promise land

A long tunnel with an open road
A foundation for a new beginning
We the Americans have a dream
To live by standards that we see free

This battle has consumed our lives
Seeking revenge due to government lies
Given no satisfaction
We intend to fight
Getting back our human rights

Plagued by virtue
Plagued by disbelief
Puncture wounds are poisoned with greed
Portrayed as illiterate
Seen all around the world
Riots of insensible size
Ravage the land of intolerable heights
Extreme conditions are being demoralized

Government shutdown forces no pay
It's been humiliated over days
We as citizens are crying shame
A nation is under disgrace

Betrayed by our government
Our visions lie dead
Betrayed by their morals
For which we cannot stand
Betrayed so coldly
We shatter our tears
Betrayed by our sins
We have no fears

Livid like a bunch of hounds
We drag our feet against the ground
Putting up a fight
Against the stupidity of life
We are stripped of all dignity
No humanity in sight
Corrupted we fight
Our virtues being left behind

Blindsided by our beliefs
We moved forward to death
A wave of blood is moving ahead
Patiently we wait, awaiting the call
Affectionate people cry out in vane
Blackened by the vision of hate

Old wounds reopen
Bullets shatter the scars
Fighting another battle
Sending patriots apart
Continuation seems nowhere to stop
Fleeing from a life of broken hearts
The bitterness is sure to be found

Buried in mud, covered in soot
Smoke obscures our views
Our existence is lately befooled
Little did we know, we would lose

Plunged deep into battle fields
Our world seems to cave
Desperately seeking victory at bay
Only forgetting our pain

Tensions give a rise
As tight spaces close in
No breathing room
No given light
We are doomed
Sadden by fright

Focusing on change
With moving ahead
Seems we are back to reality
Beating our heads
Of how we can escape
Fleeing poverty from the insane

The bitterness we cannot hide
Spewing our bodies left and right
Stress runs through our veins
Concrete illusions seem to stay

Aged over time, powerful enough
Visions of bright futures, seen floating above
Soldiers tell stories of a different tongue

Fueled by tensions greater than none

Played out like an international scene
Plunged deep into voices
Two different languages argue and agree

Nowhere to turn
Nowhere to stand
Nowhere does our world seem to blend
Four seconds too soon
The battery is running on fumes

No reason, no rhyme, no given hope
No opinion seems to withhold
No voice, no reason, no opinion
No solid ground for forgiveness
What is left to embrace?
When there is nothing in our place

A silhouette of tinted shades
A thousand words to be explained
A futuristic scene overplayed
What is left when images fade?

Nothing but a disillusion
What is left; a world of confusion.

"Revenge"

A moment passed
As the earth quaked
Bent out of shape
Does it really matter?
Where and how can it be made?

I was wondering who was insane
Nowhere does the mind roam
Back and forth through open spaces
Can you see the pain ending?
Are your senses drained or depleting?

Do we not know you?
Do we not care?
How dare you implicate us?
When nothing has compared
Revenge.

"Racist"

Two by two hung from a tree, those bastards flee
Leaving tension amongst the free
Divided ignorance and self-abuse
Send women and children drowning in booze

Men cry with blood and sweat
Southerners fuel tension between aged men
Shaking up street corners with ravage thoughts in their
heads

Intense emotions are drawn out at night
Seeking revenge on solid lines
Baseball bats give out a cry
Screams are heard throughout the fight

Vivid memories of racial hate
Distress calls are being made
Blacks and whites take their place
Leading to some hatred traits.

"Black and White"

Bold, livid and emotional,
Strong, tough, strange wicked and deranged,
Blacks and whites emanate;
Colors reflect life's giving hate.

Cried, denied and refused,
The outcome of society's blues,
Sanctions imposed, immigration takes a toll,
In a city where there is no hope.

Forced to the streets, Gangs take a beat,
Bitter, broken somewhere in between,
Intrigued by their craziness,
Reinforced by their morals,
Street fighters reign, contemplating their given hate.

Pronounced and enforced
Grounded by roots,
Written and plagued,
True colors elevate.

Cold as white, sensations roam,
Dramas plague the forbidden roads,
Sustainable by feelings, ignorant and sane,
Wasted on street corners, here lie their traits.

Frustrated and livid, democracy gives a cry,
Actual and truthful outcomes are still being denied,
Lies of tranquility seem floating astray,

Depicting illusions in many ways,
Yet remorseful issues still reign today.

"Civil War"

Coercion and deception reign amongst men
Focused on beatings with their right hands
Accused, deployed and left to hang
Is a criminal free at last?
Eviction forgiveness, no lasting stand
Freedom and progress is suppressed

Skin tough as leather makes it extreme
Hard driven forces doubt fatigue
Intrigued by their virtue
They stumble and bleed
On local streets, blood dilutes the trees
Sacrificing all that is deemed insufficient to believe

Down in the trenches, they sacrifice their lives
Fighting for vengeance, fighting for life
Divided by lines, sitting around
Families collapse on sacred grounds

Traumatized, demoted and abused
Self-inflicted are the wounds
Demoralized, sanctioned and denied
Incriminating evidence is hard to find
Trigger happy are my fellow men
Life driven happiness has no end

Suffering rage by crushing stones
Flames extinguished with no given hope
Cities in torment, governments elapse
Forgetful images are deemed to last

Bitterness ranges from street to street
Smoking guns make it unique
Ignorant attitudes self-defuse
Calling out for everlasting feuds
Faults denied, officials cried
Hatred plays their minds

Criminals freed by the vast
Concrete footprints no longer last
Where once was a post,
Now only holds sacrifices to be told
Illusions of grander, fields torn apart,
Dramatic visions curse the town,
If quietness could talk, there would be no sound.

Isolation

"Suffered"

Suffered, emerged and denied the pleasure,
Pleaded guilty in December,
Revealed at night and was simply confused,
Detailed, traumatized and abused.

Engaged and enrolled,
Vengeance is searched,
Simple and bold,
Inspiration to the soul.

Polish humor shields the tone,
Miners and sweepers are protesting the old.
Scales on a fish, bones play the gills,
Often alone, wondering if and when
Insanity will be brought to an end.

Peace no way, abdication is the game,
No romance, function taken away,
Feared of sanctions, tears drop like rain,
Destroying their faces, leaving nothing but shame.

"Solitude"

Depression hits the waves,
Wide spread faith, amongst the pain,
Solitude has its gain.

Awoken in pain,
Playful motions deter the sane.
Reassured by a pin,
Poked yet engaged,
How dare you question the girl's upper faith?

How dare to be forgotten,
When enough has been told
Crossed and defused,
Playful motions tell the truth.

Like color it fades,
Sending one to its death,
Sensitive feelings left deeply oppressed.
Spoken, rejected and gone for days,
Lives the word of a different phrase.

"Deranged and Alone"

Twice removed,
Often left in solitude,
Playing on sanity, focusing on truth,
Dare you speak the words of worthless hate?

Do you not deny your given hate?
Is sanity your game, or is democracy your faith?
You, a torment of words, a guilty mind,
How dare the corruption, caused by your plight?

Driven by sounds of memories foretold,
Cleanse the palate of your hatred goals.
For you shall lie, deranged and alone,
Seeking one's solitude.

"A Fool's Outcry"

My emotional heart is dying
There is no room for lying
Save me from my despair
You ignorant bastard, old and gray
You dare to compare
Our futures today

I swear I would lie
To sacrifice my life
But vengeance is sought
Not a given right
Change comes with a price

Not always accepted
Not always the truth
Not worth the fight
With a monkey in sight
Given your attitude
You should lie here and die

Corrupted I may be
Defense I shall seek
But my heart still bleeds
Americanism is what I think.

Anger rages
No sense in pride
You ignorant bastard
Selfishly apply
That crooks and criminals are much alike

Caught in the middle
A rough draft ahead
Leads to a sacrificial death
No sense in testifying again

A selfish blindside
Leaves nothing behind
A guilty inside, portrays my mind
Corruption is gaining
I'm losing my life.

A towel thrown in
With a fortune to lose
Grounded by diversity
It's shocking to view
A leap of faith
In a world of fools

So tired of feeling alone
There's a tug on a rope
Never regaining consciousness
Nor even some hope
The ignorant bastard is standing alone.

"Deprived of My Senses"

Every last bit of sanity is gone
Driven out by the dark
My mind wandering in and out
Darkness takes control
Cognitive attitudes take abuse
Nerve endings seem to refuse
Sounds are like fingers, with no musical tunes
Flat, undeveloped, sunken and removed.

Dare to be heard or wiped away
Dirty lies ignite the roars
A scream sends me to a halt
My ears are open, my eyes are open
Yet deprived of my senses
Patience is overlooked, forgetting a setting or a place
Do I not have anything to embrace?

"Inner Grief"

Slow to the touch, downwards and up,
Are sensitive issues, roaming above,
Openness, creativeness and imagination give way
Settling emotions details and praise

Detached by a limb,
Our emotions run high,
Playful delightful and somewhat shallow
We seek to deny

Prescribed as medication,
Viewed as relief
Some plead insanity,
Others seek refuge in inner peace

Yet not relieved of their inner grief,
Foretold is the story,
How deeply rooted are the trees, based of our feet.

Reflections of the Dead

"Fallen Hero"

The bell tolls the morning dew
A light shadow flickers through
The streets are slightly lit
The sun is peeking through the mist
The air is slowly being felt

Barbwire rips my skin,
My lips are filled with tears
The soft green grass shields my feet
My life runs through the weeds
Desperately seeking shade from a tree
I find an oak, a mile deep
Settle down to read and weep.

Gravity pulls me in with deep concerns
Forever seems so young in a world on edge
A man's word is no longer free
Racially liberated from all anxiety
Like the corpse in front of me, I hesitate
A funeral awaits me in what way am I plagued?

Bounded by my wounds
A rescue was not endured
An outcry was feared
Confronted with tears
Sentimental feelings ease the wrath
A little rough around the edges
On a given path.

Realizing the past
I take a step back
My blood stained hands
Do not factor a stand

My heart beats like a thousand drums
Pounding out reflections of a gun
A gun that would change my life
A reason I would hide
My world is crumbing down inside

Staring death in its face
I feel my soul lifting away
I hear taps being played
Is this my decay?

Pictures like memories seem to hide
Vivid images come to my mind
I think about my lonely wife
Thriving to go home, no way could I fight?

No one seems to know my face
No one seems to know my pain
A number is my saving grace
They literally question my name
Do they not have any shame?
To poison me with blame

Torn between the ropes
I fear for my life
I hear a secret voice, tell me my time
Deep in thought, I start to cry

I knew this was the end, I could not deny
Quietness still roams as I say goodbye.

"Dean Faltz"

A country divided with no given mind
Needs to put all its prejudices aside
Setting restrictions on who can survive
Racial images are being applied
Threatening the existence of day and night

Seeking vengeance day and night
Leaves a crippled wanting to fight
A white light emerges from behind
Leaving no room for sympathetic moods
The hourglass stands still in a crowded room

Buried in a box, salvaged from a yard
A self-portrait drips with tears
A paper crumples
Little feet pitter-patter
Water flows from within
The trumpet moves them to tears
Homeboy and Wink are down on knees
Crying out for their buddy Dean
Questioning their given peace.

The choir starts to sing
The pastor gives the opening speech
He quotes a certain passage
That Dean would read:

A dream date
A movie star
A city tour, she finds her part

A profile
A given place
A soft word
She hesitates

A smile
A note
A little old
Yet writing is our secret goal
To success we shall toast.

He would ponder for hours about his goal
Thinking could an old life come to a close
A powerful movement wasted, grows old

As his soul left, I felt peace
Separated by tiny spades
He had two worlds to embrace
A solider for our saving grace
And a loving dad who is gone today

When there is no sound to be heard
What does a human mind leave behind?
Knowledge, value and a story to be told
Dean was the greatest man I ever known
A fallen comrade is laid to rest
A beautiful trumpet fades out to rest.

"What Lies Ahead"

What lies ahead in reflection of the dead?
A drop of sand
A moment in death
Deep depressing finding its way
Soft Jazz controls the wave.

Although deep down heart inside
Lies a painful night
A soft piano was heard being played
A little rhythm and blues melted away
Some blues, some souls, some drifters on a lonely road.

Drifters wondered far and wide
Searching for a jazz note
Leaving many behind
Needles and pins
Tears and fears
Focus my child as the moon settles
For the light fades, yet not disassembles
A voice spoke until its end
Tell me what lies ahead?

"Remorse"

Imagination or confusion
Illustration or illusion
For these reasons I cannot cry
I feel dead inside
Days are growing old
Pieces crumble
Enclosed by walls

Dramatization of the truth
Fenced in like an animal
Leaving nothing behind
Destroys my mind
A stick of dynamite
Cold as white
A pain my heart cannot deny
Bitterness rages from inside

I feel your pain
You ignorant vein
The words you speak
Are they true or false?
Wait what should I believe?
Clear and crisp, a nerve hits the bone
Tender words come out to play
Comprehension is not my game

Do not torment me
You insensitive flame
For I will not accept the pain

I have a burning desire
To put a bullet in my brain

Only time will tell
How my soul shall dwell
No more turning back to a world of hell

Nothing concerns me, not even my sight
An explosion lights up the sky
For I could not fear the beaming light
I knew I was going to die.

I knew my shame would create some blame
In a crazy society, was I even sane?
Selling my soul to ease my pain
To stop the bleeding, not even seen
Draining my misery
Contemplating futuristic needs

Once is enough
No regrets, no remorse
A bullet punctures
All hope is lost.

"Lost Soul"

Deeply departed loss of soul,
Only human bones wondering through,
The tangled woods of a wooden road

A depth so deep,
With dark tangled weeds,
Bones mingle as humans weep.

Described as morbid and as weak,
I hate to see, a departed light and trusted soul,
For deeply departed, there goes my soul.

"Burnt reflections"

Burnt are their reflections in the middle of the town
Lost days ago when the sun dried out
Starved from water, drained of juice
Burnt is their reflection seconds before you

Lined up to bleed, shoes thrown in between
Young and old, cry out and weep
Standing alone, waiting to die,
Suffering humans denied their rights
Plagued, deprived, smoke in their eyes,
Uprooted and parched, their liberty is denied.

A tone deep, a mile high
Dreams shattered, journeys at night
Invisible immortals take flight
Orange hues light up the sky
Forgetting the nights of loneliness cries

Forgetful images lie ahead, so many were laid to rest
Burnt are their reflections, extinguished by greed
Nowhere to turn
Nowhere to bleed

Life hearted friendships deemed goodbye
Along with illusions of a better life
Captured by day, freed by night
Freedom and progress are totally denied

Burnt are their reflections in the middle of town
Seen are their reflections on sacred grounds.

"Illusions of Innocence"

Moments of silence crept in to my head
As I stood on soil with a deep scent
Painful yet loving of what lies beneath
Ages of innocence, all seem to fade
I focused on living, sadden with fear
Home was calling, gladly I would adhere

With tears raging hard, I wiped my face
Dark as my skin, blood running straight
I staggered to believe the hidden secrets
I fought to hear as my soul was thinking
My thoughts were depleting.

Curtains

"Death to My Soul"

No way could there be two shades
For I was not afraid nor alone
An ugly shadow grew old
The emotional pain was depleting an escape

The end would be near
I knew then and there
A sea of red forms in between
Waiting for some paint
Like a blank canvas
Stares me straight

Only seen by a few
A thousand mile view
A depth so deep
I could not breathe
To delay what I have, suddenly has survived.

Fractured and defenseless
Carved into stone
A jagged point rips my skin
A vein explodes, blood drips in fear
A distress signal no one hears
Arms ripped apart
I drop to my knees
I cry out and bleed

Temperature rising
Blood screaming, ready to hurl
Death is emerging

A white light encircles my body
Portraying impressions, I could not understand
A carbon copy defines who I am.

"Captive"

Corner monkeys drain my juice
With nowhere to turn
I stand amused
Not wanting to refuse
By the strength and wisdom that had me fooled
For decades I was totally confused

As animosity sets in more
A mirror proves me wrong
A world so delicately wrong
Treats me a like a human torch.

Irritated mentally and physically
Frustrated with living and lost for words
I hesitate to see
The emotional out pour.

All my dirty secrets exposed outright
Creates such a gruesome sight
As it echoes and soars
Gravity pulls me in
Lost, scared and overwhelmed
I think I'm in hell

Painful, yet simple
I forge ahead
Incarcerated like a slave
Between structures of metal and dirt
I find myself mistreated
I am done, no more.

"Goodbye"

I hit rock bottom
Could it be true?
I thought I made it
I thought I knew

A simple saying
A simple phone call
A simple hello
A simple goodbye
I dared to cry

I do not know if I could cry
Expressing myself before I die
When the hour glass ends
My dream will end
Will you still be there?
On a given hand

I truly believe
Feelings grow old with age
Until they somehow decay
Like black hair that fades
There are no boundaries to over stay

Do not let me go
For I will die
A subtle indifference in the night
Peace, my soul, my body goes
Please do not let me go
Goodbye!

"Whispers"

A voice whispered
A dream shattered
A life crumbled
A tone deep
A mile high
A window flew open, yet why?

"Two Shades: Dark"

One moment
One second
One hand
One prayer
One answer
One definitely commands
The hour has ended
One is dead.

www.ingramcontent.com/pod-product-compliance
Lightning Source LLC
Chambersburg PA
CBHW051046030426
42339CB00006B/219